Multiple Choice Questions in Fundamentals of Programming C++

125 MCQs with Solutions

Samreen Laghari

Healthy Mind Media

ISBN-13: 978-1986347198
ISBN-10: 1986347192

1) A sequence of statements whose objective is to accomplish a task is known as a:

A. Computer Program

B. Macro

C. Class

D. None of the above

Answer: A

2) In C++, anything written in double quotes (" ") is a:

A. String

B. Variable

C. Constant

D. Macro

Answer: A

3) The output of the following C++ statement will be: cout << "20 + 8";

A. 28

B. 20 + 8

C. 20

D. 8

Answer: B

4) All of the following are used to specify comments in C++ except:

A. //

B. /* ... */

C. /? ... ?/

D. Both A & B

Answer: C

5) In C++, the identifiers Number and number refer to:

A. Same identifiers

B. Different identifiers

C. Both A & B

D. None of the above

Answer: B

6) All of the following are reserved words used in C++ except:

A. integer

B. float

C. double

D. char

Answer: A

7) Point out the legal identifier:

A. Salaried employee

B. 4th

C. Hi!

D. hourlyEmployee

Answer: D

8) Minus (-) is a:

A. Unary Operator

B. Binary Operator

C. Both A & B

D. None of the Above

Answer: C

9) static_cast<int> 9.9 evaluates to:

A. 9.0

B. 9.5

C. 9

D. 10

Answer: C

10) static_cast<double>(2 + 8) evaluates to:

A. 10

B. 10.0

C. 8.0

D. 2.0

Answer: B

11) static_cast<double>(11 / 2) evaluates to:

A. 5.5

B. 5.0

C. 5

D. 6

Answer: B

12) static_cast<char>(65) evaluates to:

A. 'a'

B. 'B'

C. 'A'

D. 'b'

Answer: C

13) The statement "cout << 33 / 4 << endl;" evaluates to:

A. 8.25

B. 8

C. 8.0

D. 9

Answer: B

14) The statement "cout << 3 + 8 * 5 << endl;" evaluates to:
A. 55
B. 43.0
C. 43
D. 55.0

Answer: C

15) To print the line, \n is used for new line, we write:
A. cout << "\n is used for new line" << endl;
B. cout << "/n is used for new line" << endl;
C. cout << "\\n is used for new line" << endl;
D. cout << \n << "is used for new line" << endl;

Answer: C

16) To terminate a statement in C++, we use:
A. Colon (:)
B. Period (.)
C. Comma (,)
D. semicolon (;)

Answer: D

17) The statement j += 8 is equivalent to:
A. j + 8
B. j = 8
C. j = j + 8
D. None of the above`

Answer: C

18) All of the following are arithmetic operators in C++ except:
A. -
B. %
C. +
D. None of the above

Answer: D

19) All of the following are compound operators in C++ except:
A. +=
B. %=
C. -=
D. /*

Answer: D

20) All of the following are relational operators in C++ except:
A. ==
B. !=
C. >
D. None of the above

Answer: D

21) 'A' <= 'a' evaluates to:
A. true
B. 'b'
C. false
D. None of the above

Answer: A

22) 8 != 8 evaluates to:
A. true
B. 1
C. false
D. None of the above

Answer: C

23) The expression "!(2<=8)" evaluates to:
A. true
B. 1
C. false
D. None of the above

Answer: C

24) The array subscript operator is:
A. [ ]
B. ||
C. { }
D. ( )

25) Identify the purpose of the following statements:

       for (int i=1; i < 20; i++)
       cout << Items[i] << endl;

A. Sets the values of elements of "item" array equal to i
B. Inputs the elements into the "item" array
C. Adds the elements of the "item" array
D. Prints the elements of "item" array

26) The statement "len = strlen("Computer Program"):
A. Stores 17 in length
B. Stores 16 in length
C. Stores 15 in length
D. Stores 19 in length

27) The declaration of a struct in C++ ends with a:
A. ;
B. ,
C. }
D.)

28) The statement "int *p, q;" declares:
A. p to be a pointer variable of type int and q to be a variable of type int
B. p and q both to be a pointer variable of type int
C. p and q both to be a variable of type int
D. p to be a variable of type int and q to be a pointer

29) In C++, when * operator is used as a unary operator, it is referred to as:
A. Dereferecing operator
B. Indirection operator
C. Both A & B
D. Multiplication operator

Answer: C

30) _____ **operator does not take non-integer operands:**
A. +
B. -
C. *
D. %

Answer: D

31) Interchanging the equality operator (==) with assignment operator(=) results in:
A. Syntax Error
B. Logical Error
C. Execution Error
D. None of the above

Answer: B

32) In an if statement, placing a semicolon immediately after the right parenthesis results in:
A. Syntax Error
B. Logical Error
C. Execution Error
D. None of the above

Answer: B

33) Execution of a C++ program begins from:
A. #include statement
B. main function
C. User-defined functions
D. None of the above

Answer: B

34) To document a program and improve its readability in C++, we use:
A. Functions
B. Classes
C. Comments
D. Operators

Answer: C

35) Specifying an identifier with the same name as a C++ keyword results in:
A. No error
B. Logical Error
C. Syntax Error
D. Execution Error

Answer: C

36) Attempting to divide by zero results in a:
A. Fatal Error
B. Syntax Error
C. Logical Error
D. None of the above

Answer: A

37) A function defined in another function results in:
A. Syntax Error
B. Logical Error
C. Execution Error
D. None of the above

Answer: A

38) A consecutive group of memory locations having same name and type is known as:
A. Heap
B. Queue
C. Array
D. Stack

Answer: C

39) Referring to an element outside the array bounds results in:

A. Syntax Error

B. Execution Time Logical Error

C. Exception

D. None of the above

Answer: B

40) Which of the following is not a C++ operator:

A. new

B. delete

C. sizeof

D. private

Answer: D

41) In C++, which of the following string function breaks a string into tokens:

A. strlen

B. strtok

C. strcpy

D. strcmp

Answer: B

42) In C++, which of the following string function takes a string as an argument and returns the number of characters contained in it:

A. strlen

B. strtok

C. strcpy

D. strcmp

Answer: A

43) In C++, which of the following string function compares the first string argument with the second string argument character by character:
A. strlen
B. strtok
C. strcpy
D. strcmp

Answer: D

44) In C++, which of the following string function copies the second argument string into its first argument string:
A. strlen
B. strtok
C. strcpy
D. strcmp

Answer: C

45) In C++, which of the following string functions appends its second string argument to its first string argument:
A. strtok
B. strcpy
C. strcmp
D. strcat

Answer: D

46) A variable that contains the address of another variable is known as:
A. Array
B. Pointer
C. Function
D. String

Answer: B

47) In C++, the pointer dereferencing operator is:
A. !
B. *
C. .
D. &

Answer: B

48) Using logical AND operator (&&) in place of bitwise AND operator (&) results in:
A. Syntax Error
B. Logical Error
C. Execution Error
D. None of the above

Answer: B

49) In C++, all preprocessor directives start with:
A. +
B. #
C. $
D. %

Answer: B

50) A preprocessor directive to create symbolic constants and macros is:
A. #include
B. #define
C. #undef
D. #if

Answer: B

51) Size of char in C++ is:
A. 4 bytes
B. 1 byte
C. 2 bytes
D. 8 bytes

Answer: B

52) Size of an int in C++ is:
A. 4 bytes
B. 1 byte
C. 2 bytes
D. 8 bytes

Answer: A

53) Size of long int in C++ is:
A. 4 bytes
B. 1 byte
C. 2 bytes
D. 8 bytes

Answer: A

54) Size of float in C++ is:
A. 4 bytes
B. 1 byte
C. 2 bytes
D. 8 bytes

Answer: A

55) Size of double in C++ is:
A. 4 bytes
B. 1 byte
C. 2 bytes
D. 8 bytes

Answer: D

56) A loop that executes at least once is a:
A. for loop
B. do...while loop
C. while loop
D. None of the above

Answer: B

57) An operator that can be used to replace an "if...else" statement is:

A. .*

B. ?:

C. /=

D. +=

Answer: B

58) All of the following are file opening modes in C++, except:

A. ios::ate

B. ios::in

C. ios::out

D. None of the above

Answer: D

59) A data type in C++, which can only assume two values i.e. true or false:

A. int

B. double

C. float

D. bool

Answer: D

60) In C++, a word frequently used in place of error is:

A. Failure

B. Mistake

C. Bug

D. None of the above

Answer: C

61) A type provided directly by C++ is known as:

A. User-defined type

B. Built-in type

C. Explicit Type

D. None of the above

Answer: B

62) Declaring a function parameter to be a reference refers to as:
A. call-by-value
B. call-by-reference
C. Pass-by-value
D. None of the above

Answer: B

63) Passing a copy of parameter to the called function refers to as:
A. Pass-by-value
B. call-by-reference
C. Pass-by-reference
D. None of the above

Answer: A

64) Declaring an entity that is defined somewhere else can be accomplished using:
A. define keyword
B. extern keyword
C. include keyword
D. using keyword

Answer: B

65) A stream attached to a file is known as a file stream and is represented as:
A. ifstream
B. ofstream
C. fstream
D. All of the above

Answer: D

66) Which of the following is a ternary operator (takes three operands)?

A. .*

B. +=

C. ?:

D. >=

Answer: C

67) The number 630.56 can be represented using:

A. int

B. char

C. float

D. bool

Answer: C

68) All of the given assignment statements are valid except:

A. x = 20;

B. 48 = t;

C. r = 2.2;

D. Grade = 'A';

Answer: B

69) A cout statement in the following that contains error is:

A. cout << "Fundamentals of Programming" << endl;

B. cout << "\nFundamentals of Programming" << endl;

C. cout << "\n Fundamentals of Programmimg \n;

D. cout << Fundamentals of Programming << endl;

Answer: D

70) The negation operator (~) is a:

A. unary operator

B. binary operator

C. ternary operator

D. None of the above

Answer: A

71) The expression "48 / 4 - 10" evaluates to:
A. 2
B. 8
C. -8
D. -2

Answer: A

72) The expression "(3 + 20) * 10" evaluates to:
A. 203
B. 230
C. -230
D. -203

Answer: B

73) Assuming x=20, the expression (20 <= x + 8) evaluates to:
A. True
B. false
C. zero
D. None of the above

Answer: A

74) Correct syntax for passing an array to a function as an argument is:
A. Heapsort(&arr);
B. Heapsort(#arr);
C. Heapsort(*arr);
D. Heapsort(arr[]);

Answer: A

75) User-defined C++ header files have:
A. .cpp extension
B. .h extension
C. .a extension
D. .c extension

Answer: B

76) In C++, a new **seed** can be set for the random number generator by the function:
A. rand()
B. srand()
C. random()
D. seed()

Answer: B

77) setfill() is a function of:
A. <iostream>
B. <iomanip>
C. <cstdio>
D. <ios>

Answer: B

78) In C++, a string can be converted into a floating point number using:
A. atoi() function
B. atof() function
C. atol() function
D. atoll() function

Answer: B

79) cerr is included in:
A. <iostream>
B. <iomanip>
C. <cstdio>
D. <cstdlib>

Answer:A

80) clog is a member of:
A. <iostream>
B. <iomanip>
C. <cstdio>
D. <cstdlib>

Answer: A

81) getchar() is a function of:
A. <iostream>
B. <iomanip>
C. <cstdio>
D. <cstdlib>

Answer: C

82) A function to test if the passed integer argument corresponding to an ASCII character is an uppercase letter is:
A. toupper()
B. tolower()
C. isupper()
D. islower()

Answer: C

83) C++ was developed by:
A. Martin Richards
B. Bjarne Stroustrup
C. Ken Thompson
D. Donald E. Knuth

Answer: B

84) The C++ operator used for input is known as:
A. Stream Insertion operator
B. Stream Extraction operator
C. cin operator
D. Input operator

Answer: B

85) The C++ operator used for output is known as:
A. Stream Insertion operator
B. Stream Extraction operator
C. cout operator
D. Output operator

Answer: A

86) Point out the correct way of declaring a pointer:
A. int *p;
B. int* p;
C. int   p*;
D. Both A & B

Answer: D

87) The abs() function that returns the absolute value of an integer is a function of:
A. <cmath>
B. <cstdlib>
C. <cstdio>
D. <ctime>

Answer: B

88) The sqrt() function that returns the square root of a number is a function of:
A. <cmath>
B. <cstdlib>
C. <cstdio>
D. <ctime>

Answer: A

89) The div() function that returns the integral quotient and remainder of the number is a function of:
A. <cmath>
B. <cstdlib>
C. <cstdio>
D. <ctime>

Answer: B

90) The C++ operator used for accessing a namespace is:
A. ;
B. ::
C. #
D. .

Answer: C

91) The starting index of arrays in C++ is:

A. 1

B. 0

C. 2

D. 3

Answer: B

92) In C++, to access the 10th element in an array of size 10, we specify:

A. Arr[10];

B. Arr[9];

C. Arr[0];

D. None of the above

Answer: B

93) Assuming the Boolean variables named empty and full with values empty = true and full = false, the result of the following expression will be:

$$!((empty \mid\mid full) \&\& (empty \&\& full))$$

A. true

B. false

C. zero

D. None of the above

Answer: A

94) The number of parameter(s), srand() function takes is/are:

A. 3

B. 4

C. 1

D. 2

Answer: C

95) The function call "rand() % 50" will generate:
A. 0
B. 50
C. 49
D. Any number between 0 and 49

Answer: D

96) The scope of a global variable in C++ is:
A. Inside the function in which it is declared
B. Outside all functions of the program
C. Inside a code block
D. None of the above

Answer: B

97) The scope of a local variable in C++ is:
A. Inside the function in which it is declared
B. Inside a code block
C. Both A & B
D. None of the above

Answer: C

98) Which of the following statement generates random numbers between 1 and 100:
A. rand() % 100
B. rand() % 100 +1
C. rand() % 1 + 100
D. None of the above

Answer: B

99) A pointer in a structure in C++ can be accessed using:
A. . operator
B. -> operator
C. .* operator
D. None of the above

Answer: B

100) The members of a structure in C++ can be accessed using:
A. . operator
B. -> operator
C. .* operator
D. None of the above

Answer: A

101) The bitwise left shift operator in C++ is represented by the symbol:
A. <
B. <<
C. >>
D. None of the above

Answer: B

102) The bitwise OR operator in C++ is represented by the symbol:
A. |
B. ||
C. OR
D. None of the above

Answer: A

103) The <iostream> object used to display information on the screen is:
A. cin
B. cout
C. std
D. None of the above

Answer: B

104) The preprocessor directive that is used to insert the contents of another file into the C++ program is :
A. #define
B. #include
C. #ifndef
D. None of the above

Answer: B

105) An alternative name for a constant in C++ is:
A. Variable
B. Literal
C. Integer
D. None of the above

Answer: B

106) Part of a C++ program that has access to a variable is known as its
A. Scope
B. Range
C. Value
D. None of the above

Answer: A

107) The <iostream> object used to read data from the keyboard is:
A. cin
B. cout
C. std
D. input

Answer: A

108) Assuming a=2 and b=33, the result of the expression "static_cast<double>(b) / static_cast<double>(a)" will be:
A. 16
B. 16.5
C. 17
D. None of the above

Answer: B

109) All of the following are manipulators in <iomanip> except:
A. showpoint
B. setprecision
C. setw
D. None of the above

Answer: D

110) An operator used to compare numeric and char values is known as a:

A. Conditional operator

B. Relational operator

C. Compound operator

D. None of the above

Answer: B

111) A boolean or integer variable used to specify that a certain condition has met is known as a:

A. flag

B. Conditional variable

C. Functional Variable

D. None of the above

Answer: A

112) The C++ operator that adds 1 to its operand is:

A. ++

B. +

C. +=

D. None of the above

Answer: A

113) The C++ operator that subtracts 1 from its operand is:

A. -

B. -=

C. --

D. None of the above

Answer: C

114) A variable that increments or decrements along with the iteration of a loop is known as a:

A. Literal

B. Counter

C. Constant

D. None of the above

Answer: B

115) All of the following are pre-test loops except:
A. do . . . while loop
B. for loop
C. while loop
D. None of the above

Answer: A

116) A counter variable in a C++ program that needs to remember its state will be declared:
A. const
B. static
C. auto
D. None of the above

Answer: B

117) A statement that causes a loop to terminate early is:
A. switch
B. continue
C. break
D. None of the above

Answer: C

118) A C++ program may be broken up into small manageable functions called:
A. Objects
B. Structures
C. Classes
D. Modules

Answer: D

119) Dividing a C++ program into smaller and more manageable units is referred to as :
A. Object Oriented Programming
B. Declarative Programming
C. Modular Programming
D. None of the above

Answer: C

120) The name of an array can be treated as a constant:
A. Variable
B. Pointer
C. Function
D. None of the above

Answer: B

121) Performing mathematical operations on pointers is known as:
A. Pointer Casting
B. Pointer Manipulation
C. Pointer Arithmetic
D. None of the above

Answer: C

122) A string function that searches for a string inside another string is:
A. strstr
B. strcat
C. strcmp
D. strcpy

Answer: A

123) A string function that accepts a CString and converts it into an int is:
A. atof()
B. atoi()
C. atol()
D. None of the above

Answer: B

124) The concept of placing a structure variable inside another structure as a member is referred to as a:
A. Nested Structure
B. Nested Loop
C. All of the above
D. None of the above

Answer: A

125) A pointer that is still pointing to the memory location whose memory has been deallocated is known as a:
A. Dangling Pointer
B. Null Pointer
C. Void Pointer
D. None of the above

Answer: A

Index

www.ingramcontent.com/pod-product-compliance
Lightning Source LLC
Chambersburg PA
CBHW070907070326
40690CB00009B/2026